The Highlands of Scotland

Books by W. A. Poucher
available from Constable

Scotland
Wales
The Lake District
The magic of Skye
The Scottish Peaks
The Peak and Pennines
The Lakeland Peaks
The Welsh Peaks

Other books now out of print

The backbone of England
Climbing with a camera
Escape to the hills
A camera in the Cairngorms
Scotland through the lens
Highland holiday
The North Western Highlands
Lakeland scrapbook
Lakeland through the lens
Lakeland holiday
Lakeland journey
Over lakeland fells
Wanderings in Wales
Snowdonia through the lens
Snowdon holiday
Peak panorama
The Surrey hills
The magic of the Dolomites
West country journey
Journey into Ireland

Liathach

(frontispiece)

Spidean a'Choire Leith is the highest of the seven tops crowning the five-mile summit ridge of this magnificent mountain. The picture shows the view from it to the east, with the rising ridge in the foreground, and Beinn Eighe in the distance.

THE HIGHLANDS OF SCOTLAND

W. A. Poucher

Constable London

First published in Great Britain 1983
by Constable and Company Limited
10 Orange Street London WC2H 7EG
Copyright © 1983 by W. A. Poucher
ISBN 0 09 464980 4
Text filmset by Servis Filmsetting Ltd, Manchester
Printed and bound in Japan by
Dai Nippon Company, Tokyo

The photographs

Preface

In 1980 Constable published *Scotland*, my first book in colour: in it I included such scenes of the country's rugged grandeur as appealed to my eye and camera. The photographs were studies of the glens and bens at their best, rather than just passing snapshots. If you ask, 'When *do* they look their best?' the answer is, 'When the sunlight illuminates them to perfection.' As the direction of the sun's beams varies throughout the day, and as there is only one moment when the light is at the best angle to display each particular object, it follows that a great deal of patience is needed to capture the perfect shot.

When I chose the photographs for *Scotland*, I selected those which I hoped would please both the Scots, who are justly proud of their country, and the thousands of tourists who visit them. In this, judging by the enthusiasm of the reviewers, I succeeded. However, there was one adverse criticism – from my fellow mountaineers. They felt that on the whole I had omitted shots taken from the ridges and pinnacles they negotiate, shots which reveal the spectacular views that only mountaineers can revel in.

In this book, therefore, I have included many studies which share the breath-taking world of the rock-climber with the chairbound and the walker. The pictures may be considered less beautiful than wide views of the glens, but they are certainly more dramatic. Compare, for instance, An Teallach as seen in plate 104/5 of *Scotland* with plates 51, 52, and 53 in this book.

As Skye is my favourite island, and a magnet for mountaineers, I have included a few pictures of the Coolins, the finest mountain range in Britain. Many mountain walkers have asked me to detail a safe, easy walking route to the main ridge of the Coolins. It is generally accepted that Bruach na Frithe is the best of all viewpoints, and one that is easily reached; but I offer in these pages an alternative route by way of Sgurr nan Gobhar, which is perhaps an easier climb since the path to it rises gently from the youth hostel in Glen Brittle. After passing the cairn on this peak, the ridge leading up to Sgurr na Banachdich is a super striding edge, where any difficult bits can be turned safely, and where the views of wild corries on either side maintain interest right up to the main ridge. As regards climbing the peaks portrayed in this book, I refer readers to my *Scottish Peaks* which contains full details, with photographs, of the safe ascent of them all.

The photographs in this book are arranged in order from south to north and south again, to help the traveller to follow my tour of the most splendid scenery that the Highlands of Scotland has to offer.

W. A. Poucher
4 Heathfield
Reigate Heath
Surrey
1983

The view from North Goat Fell

Brodick and Corrie are the starting-points for the easy ascent of Goat Fell, the highest peak in the Isle of Arran. A pinnacled ridge runs due north from its summit, and has no problems for the mountain walker: from North Goat Fell this spectacular view can be seen. It includes three important features of the central ridge which are, from left to right: Cir Mnor, with its many varied rock-climbs; the Peak of the Castles, a fine belvedere for the walker; and the Carlin's Leap, a hiatus in the distant ridge whose difficult crossing should be left to the rock-climber. The broad ridge in the foreground is notorious for its slippery granite sand: it falls to

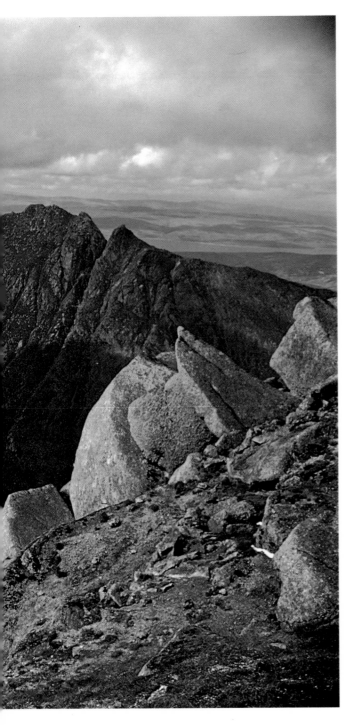

Coich na h'Oighe

(overleaf)

Rising at the northern end of the Goat Fell ridge, with the Punch Bowl on its right, this opens up a splendid prospect of the Firth of Clyde. Though the ridge is less popular with rock-climbers than the nearby Cir Mhor, walkers should not attempt to traverse it.

the saddle which separates Glen Rosa on the left from Glen Sannox on the right.

Ben Lui and Beinn a'Chleibh

These two mountains dominate the southern slopes of Glen Lochy, and their traverse from Tyndrum to Dalmally makes an exhilarating walk.

The north ridge of Ben Lui

(overleaf)

The ascent of this airy ridge is perhaps the most interesting route to the summit of Ben Lui. The only problem is to reach it, despite its proximity to a car-park on the other side of both a river and a railway line. When the river is low, climbers can ford it, but when they cross the railway line they are trespassing. At present both river and rail can be crossed by a bridge two miles down the glen. Climbers who have known Ben Lui for years will note the rapid growth of Glenlochy Forest along its lower slopes.

Ben Cruachan from Loch Awe

Ben Cruachan is the highest of the eight tops crowning this great mountain range, which is bounded on the north by the deep rift of Glen Noe and on the south by Loch Awe and the Pass of Brander. It covers an area about twenty miles square and forms a horseshoe stretching some four miles from east to west. The long walk along these lofty ridges is one of the finest in this part of Scotland.

The *summit of*
Ben Cruachan
from the *reservoir*

(overleaf)

This sheet of water occupies the floor of Coire Cruachan, and its dam wall may be reached by a three-mile walk along a well-made road. From there the ascent of Ben Cruachan is made by first scaling the slopes of Meall Cuanail, seen in this photograph on the left of the summit, and finishing with a short, steep climb.

Glen Orchy falls

A single-track road with passing places leaves
Glen Lochy near Dalmally to make a shorter
connection with the highway across Rannoch
Moor, and it follows the burn all the way.
There is a large lay-by opposite the falls, which
are the finest hereabouts.

Black Rock Cottage

(overleaf)

This well-placed hut, owned by the Ladies'
Scottish Climbing Club, lies beneath the
terminal peaks of the Blackmount near the
cable-car station about a mile to the south-east
of Kingshouse. Members of this famous club
grant reciprocal rights to other clubs, a
privilege much appreciated by visiting climbers.
The hut commands wide views of Rannoch
Moor and the peaks of Glencoe – Buachaille
Etive Mor is seen in the background of this
photograph.

Stob Dubh from Dalness

Standing at the south-western end of the summit ridge of Buachaille Etive Beag, this peak commands one of the finest vistas of Glen Etive. To the west of it lies the Lairig Eilde and to the east the Lairig Gartain, two low passes which connect Glencoe with Glen Etive, from which it may be climbed.

Buachaille Etive Mor

(overleaf)

This photograph shows the north face, which offers rock-climbing routes of every grade of difficulty in both summer and winter. Experienced mountain walkers, though, can reach the summit of Stob Dearg from Altnafeadh by way of Coire na Tulaich.

Glencoe from the old road

This photograph displays the Three Sisters of Glencoe to perfection, but it does not reveal the summit of Bidean nam Bian which is hidden behind the slopes of Beinn Fhada on the left. The conspicuous top on the right, which is often mistaken for it, is in fact Stob Coire nan Lochan.

The summit of Bidean nam Bian

(overleaf)

Since this peak, which dominates the great range bearing its name, cannot be seen from the road in Glencoe, only the climber who ascends the adjoining peak of Stob Coire nam Beith can view the crowning glory of Argyll, as seen in this picture. Also disclosed are the Diamond and Church Door buttresses at its base on the left, both of them favourites with rock-climbers.

Aonach Eagach from Loch Achtriochtan

This narrow ridge forms the north wall of Glencoe, and a two-mile section of it affords one of the most sensational traverses in the Central Highlands. This begins at Am Bodach, seen on the extreme right of this photograph, and ends at Stob Coire Leith, just out of the picture on the left. Care must be taken all the way, but particularly when descending Am Bodach for Meall Dearg, the highest top on this section of the ridge.

Looking west along the ridge

(overleaf)

The well-worn path, which indicates the popularity of this traverse, did not exist in my early days, when a climber would often encounter ptarmigan and their chicks on Aonach Eagach's lonely crest.

The last pinnacle

This shot was taken in retrospect: crossing this
pinnacle in wet weather needs the utmost care.

The ridge from
Stob Coire Leith

(overleaf)

This photograph gives a complete view of the whole Aonach Eagach ridge, known also (because of its many undulations) as the Notched Ridge. The descent to the glen is made from the col below Sgor nam Fiannaidh, over steep grass all the way.

Bidean nam Bian from Loch Leven

Many beautiful scenes are unveiled from the
road along the north side of Loch Leven – this
one is perhaps the best.

Corran Ferry

(overleaf)

There is a regular service across the narrows of Loch Linnhe, and beyond the houses in Corran rise the hills about Loch Sunart, dominated by the great peak of Garbh Bheinn of Ardgour. Climbers bound for the mountain should take the improved road that runs along the coast to Inversanda, six miles from the ferry, and park their cars where a small section of the old road has been left untouched.

Garbh Bheinn on a wild day

A seven-mile walk over the group starts at the bridge across the burn flowing down Glen Iubhair. The route circles the Glen, and by walking to the right of it, uphill to Druim an Iubhair and its lochan, a splendid prospect of the peak is revealed. This shot was taken on a wild day, but the side-lighting clearly shows the Great Gully, perhaps the finest and most difficult rock-climb on the mountain, and one of the last major gullies in the Scottish Highlands to be conquered.

Sunlight
reveals all

(overleaf)

Taken on a brighter day than the previous photograph, this picture shows to perfection the grandeur of Garbh Bheinn, whose traverse runs along its skyline from right to left, crossing Sgor Mhic Eacharna and Bheinn Bheag before dropping down to Bealach Feith'n Amean and its lochan (right of picture). Above this the precipitous northern slopes of the peak rise abruptly, and the summit cairn opens up one of the finest panoramas in Ardgour, with all the mountains from Ben Nevis to Beinn a'Bheithir spread out on the other side of Loch Linnhe. The descent starts by crossing the rocky dip on the ridge to Sron a'Gharbh Choire Bhig, and continues downhill (left of picture), skirting the slabby outcrops all the way to the bridge.

Ben Resipol

The prominence of this mountain, which is seen here from the narrow terminus of Loch Shiel, is owing to its relative isolation on low ground between Lochs Shiel and Sunart. Though it can be climbed from many directions, the approach to it from Resipol Farm on Loch Sunart is the most popular.

Glen Nevis

(overleaf)

The drive from Fort William to the head of this glen is one of the most beautiful in Scotland, and opens up some glorious views of the precipitous southern front of the Ben (on the left) and of the Mamores (on the right).

An Gearanach

The upper reaches of Glen Nevis, together with
this mountain and Steall Waterfall, can be seen
by those who leave their cars in the car-park
near the head of the glen, and take the path
leading from it.

Aonach Mor
and Ben Nevis

(overleaf)

The Ben and its satellites can best be seen by afternoon light at Banavie, from the road to Loch Lochy.

Glenfinnan

The drive from Fort William to Mallaig,
perhaps the most picturesque in Lochaber,
passes the Prince Charlie monument at
Glenfinnan. Most travellers photograph this
with Loch Sheil in the background: this shot,
taken looking the other way, reveals the
curving railway viaduct, with a train crossing it
on the way to Mallaig.

Loch Eilt

(overleaf)

This loch, one of the most beautiful in
Lochaber, is reached from Glenfinnan by a hilly
road close by the railway. In my early days, the
small islet in the narrows of Loch Eilt had
seven fine trees: in the intervening years these
have disappeared one by one in the westerly
gales, and now it is barren.

Gairich

In my previous book, *Scotland*, I enthused about the scenic drive from Invergarry to Loch Hourn. As many readers have asked for more photographs of this, I include here five pictures that appeal to me. Gairich comes into view after passing Tomdoun, and from there it seems to stand at the head of Loch Poulary. In fact, it rises on the south side of the Loch Quoich reservoir, as this picture, taken from the road above the dam, shows.

Loch Quoich

(overleaf)

The road keeps to the loch's northern shore for miles; this photograph was taken about halfway along the immense stretch of water, fully revealing the splendour of its situation.

Sgurr na Ciche

This magnificent mountain, the highest in the
group of peaks that surrounds Loch Nevis, was
taken with a telephoto lens from nearly the
same viewpoint as the previous picture. The
starting point for the climb to Sgurr na Ciche
can be reached by a long tramp from the foot
of Loch Quoich, but is attained more easily by
boat from Mallaig to the village of Inverie.

Strange horses

The first time I took this drive to Loch Hourn, these horses were standing motionless as I passed, and on my return some hours later, they had not moved an inch. On my second visit, a few days later, I found them on the shore of Loch Hourn, motionless as before.

In the foothills

(overleaf)

On leaving Loch Quoich the narrow road winds in and out among the foothills, and at every turn reveals a dramatic change of scene, with plenty of subjects to attract the alert photographer. This shot is one that appealed to me.

The Five Sisters of Kintail

(overleaf pp 74/75)

This magnificent range dominates the head of Loch Duich, and this photograph, taken some years ago from the crest of Mam Rattachan, shows their finest elevation, as well as including the blue of the loch. Today, the trees in the foreground have grown so high that the peaks on the right of the picture only just overtop them. The complete traverse of this long range is a considerable undertaking, even with transport to a point in Glen Shiel immediately below the Bealach an Lapain, where the east-to-west route begins. If completed, it involves 10,000 feet of ascent and descent: the pictures that follow will give the non-climbing reader some idea of this lofty terrain.

Sgurr na Ciste Duibhe

This rocky peak appears ahead of the climber
after the long ascent of Sgurr nan Spainteach,
and its crossing in wild weather requires special
care. This picture is interesting because of the
distant prospect of the saddle and its adjoining
Sgurr na Forcan, which stand on the far side of
the glen.

The famous view from Sgurr Fhuaran

(overleaf)

This is the highest peak in the group, and on a clear day it affords one of the most celebrated panoramas in Scotland. As seen in this photograph, the dome of Ben Nevis rises in the south-east above the complex skyline of peaks and ridges.

The cliffs of Saighead

From the next bealach rises the triple-headed
peak of Sgurr nan Saighead, whose cliffs fall
precipitously into the depths of Gleann Lichd
on the right.

Beinn Bhan

The satellites of this mountain rise spectacularly above Loch Kishorn, but the four castellated corries facing the north-east, and seen only distantly from the narrow road to Shieldaig, are its finest feature, and well worth a close inspection. To reach them easily, follow the stalkers' path which starts beyond the river-bridge at Tornapress and skirts the south-east shoulder of the mountain. When the corries appear high up on the left, walk up to them over the heathery slopes that lead to Coire na Feola, which is seen in this picture.

Shieldaig
from afar

(overleaf)

During the early stages of the steep drive to Kenmore, there are several viewpoints on the right which admirably reveal this charming village. I took this picture with a long-focus lens.

Beinn Alligin

Known to mountaineers as the 'Jewel of Torridon', this peak is the most westerly of the three great mountains that grace the glen of that name. It offers no special problems to the experienced mountain walker, except possibly the crossing of the three Horns, and most climbers on reaching Torridon will probably tackle it first.

Sgurr Mhor
and the Horns

(overleaf)

To reach this viewpoint, the climber leaves the car-park and ascends the heathery slopes on the other side of the road, then walks to the left along the shoulder of the mountain to the mouth of Coire an Laoigh. This spot gives a nearer view of Sgurr Mhor and its 1,800-foot gash, together with a detailed frontal view of the Horns.

The summit panorama

From the summit cairn of Sgurr Mhor there is a superb panorama, as seen here. Immediately below are the Horns, then comes Beinn Dearg, topped by the higher ridges of Beinn Eighe. Though special care is needed in the ascent of the first Horn, all of them can be turned by walking along the path below them, which leads downhill all the way to the stalkers' path in the glen.

Alligin after a storm

Shortly before I took this photograph I was
walking along the path in Coire Mhic Nobuil
when a storm broke over the mountain, and
soon afterwards the water rushed down in
torrents from Toll a'Mhadaidh. In the
background, against the clearing sky, is the
summit with the Horns on its right.

Liathach from Inver Alligin

From this little hamlet nestling on the shore of
Loch Torridon, immediately below Beinn
Alligin, there is an outstanding view of the
'end-on' prospect of Liathach.

Liathach from Glen Torridon

(overleaf)

This is the most imposing view of Liathach, which rises ahead suddenly as one is passing Loch Clair on the drive from Kinlochewe to Torridon. Its cliffs of sandstone, stretching as far as the eye can see, at first seem unclimbable. But once the car-park a little further along this road is reached (where the driver of the van in the picture could easily have turned around), a well-worn track can be picked out, ending at the steep gully on the face of Stuc a'Choire Dhuibh Bhig.

Looking west along the summit ridge

Many climbers now like to make the exciting traverse of Liathach, whose summit ridge is some five miles long, and has seven well-defined tops of which the highest, Spidean a'Choire Leith, is clearly seen in this photograph. Looking the other way (frontispiece), there is a superb view of Beinn Eighe. Though the traverse has no problems in summer, the large blocks of quartzite on the summit are very sharp, and require care.

West from Spidean

From the summit cairn, this is the view of the
continuation of the Liathach ridge as far as
Mullach an Rathain: as can be seen, its traverse
is more difficult. The crux is the passing of Am
Fasarinen, whose pinnacles demand of the
climber a steady head, for the drops on its right
are vertical. (The pinnacles can be turned on the
left by a track below them.) From Spidean
Choire Leith there is a vast panorama with a
ring of peaks in every direction except the west,
where the climber sees the coastline and the
glittering sea.

Beinn Eighe from Loch Coulin

(overleaf)

This great mountain, by far the largest of the
Torridon peaks, is a complete range in itself.
While its eastern aspect is best seen from
Kinlochewe, the long southern front appears at
its most impressive from Loch Coulin, just to
the south of Loch Clair. This shot was taken in
May, after a three-day blizzard.

The summit ridge of Beinn Eighe

This picture, showing the undulations of the ridge (which present no difficulties to the experienced climber), was taken from the cairn on Sgurr an Fhir Duibhe which stands at the sharp north-to-west bend in the ridge. On the left rises Liathach, and on the right the first peak is Sgurr Ban.

Coire Mhic Fhearchair

(overleaf)

The traverse of Beinn Eighe continues without difficulty and ends at its highest top – Ruadh-stac Mor, which dominates the most dramatic scene on the whole range. Coire Mhic Fhearchair faces the north-west and is considered the finest corrie in all Scotland, with the best rock-climbing in Torridon. Three immense buttresses support the top, their lower halves consisting of sandstone and their upper ones of quartzite, with a lonely lochan at their feet. Mountain walkers can reach this magnificent corrie by one of two paths: from Grudie Bridge on Loch Maree or from Glen Torridon by a path starting from the car-park. A good photograph must take advantage of the light which floods the corrie only at 8 pm on a summer evening.

Slioch

Standing in splendid isolation to the north of the headwaters of Loch Maree, this mountain attracts attention by virtue of its bold, square, castellated summit. The only problem in ascending it is the long tramp round the head of the loch from Kinlochewe to Glen Bianasdail at its base. This can be shortened by crossing the river at Taagan, or by arranging for a ghillie to row the climber across the loch and pick him up again later. To the east of Slioch's summit is a small corrie famous for its alpines in spring.

Toll an Lochain

(overleaf)

An Teallach is one of the most spectacular mountains in the Highlands and vies in splendour with Liathach in Torridon. Its main ridge, some three miles long, throws out three spurs to the east: these enclose two magnificent corries, of which Toll an Lochain is pictured here. The photograph, taken in early morning light, clearly shows the steepness of its cliffs, the serrated skyline ridge, and the lochan nearly 2,000 feet below. The traverse of the ridge goes from right to left, and the skyline peaks in that order are: Sgurr Fiona, Lord Berkeley's Seat, Corrag Bhuidhe Pinnacles, and Corrag Bhuide Buttress.

The summit ridge of An Teallach

This shot, taken from the adjoining Bidean
'Ghlas Thuill, the dominating summit of An
Teallach, throws into prominence the pinnacles
on the ridge, which are named (from right to
left) in the previous caption.

Corrag Bhuidhe

(overleaf)

Beyond Sgurr Fiona, this spectacular sandstone
ridge narrows, with abysmal drops on the left
and steep slopes on the right, before rising to
the dizzy eminence of Lord Berkeley's Seat
which overhangs the corrie. Beyond that again,
the ridge rises steeply to the first of the four
Corrag Bhuidhe pinnacles: these are all
surrounded by terrific chasms, but are without
comparison on this mountain for the views they
offer of the whole ridge, together with Beinn
Dearg Mhor on the other side of the wide
Strath na Sheallag. The rest of the ridge is not
difficult, and the descent can be made by Cadha
Gobhlach, where a stone shoot descends to the
lochan shore.

The approach to Stac Polly

(overleaf pp 116/117)

Fourteen miles from Ullapool, this little
Coigach peak stands alone above the waters of
Loch Lurgain, and is reached by a single-track
road that turns left at Drumrunie from the main
highway to Ledmore. There are distant views of
the mountain long before the turn, but only on
approaching the loch is its elevation seen to full
advantage, as in this, my favourite, picture of it.

Climbing the peak

There is a car-park immediately below Stac Polly, and from it was taken this picture of two youngsters and their parents starting the ascent. There is a zigzag track on its northern slope, but most climbers take the talus slope direct and soon reach the saddle. This little peak delights photographers, since the summit ridge offers many subjects with exciting foregrounds and distant views of scattered blue lochans.

Looking west along the ridge

(overleaf)

From the saddle the eastern top of Stac Polly is easily reached, and it discloses a good view of the ridge with its ragged southern slope, as seen here.

Cul Mor appears above the cliffs

(overleaf p 121)

From a southern spur near the end of the summit ridge of Stac Polly some of the best views are obtained by looking back – the riven cliffs, seen in this picture, overtopped by the distant peak of Cul Mor.

Suilven from the western towers

(overleaf pp 122/123)

From the same vantage-point as the previous picture, the climber can look north and see Suilven between the two imposing western towers.

Climbers on the northern pinnacles

he pinnacles on the northern slopes of Stac
olly are nothing like as spectacular as those on
e south – far less sharp, and indeed often flat-
pped, as seen here, though they drop sheer
veral hundred feet to the scree. From this side
f the ridge there is a superb view of the
mmense blue stretch of Loch Sionascaig.

Looking back late in the day

(overleaf)

The climber must visit Stac Polly towards
sundown to capture a shot like this, when the
rays of the setting sun paint the mountain with
gold. This was taken during the descent to
Linneraineach.

Suilven from Elphin

Suilven is wedge-shaped, and rises in splendid isolation from the lochan-strewn moors of Sutherland. Seen here from the east, near Cam Loch, it presents a sharp, tapering and inaccessible appearance, whereas from the west near Lochinver its lofty summit is rounded (see plate 121 in *Scotland*). Its summit ridge is one and a half miles long, and climbers must walk about five miles to reach the gully that gives easy access to the Bealach Mor, where the traverse begins.

The long ridge from the south
(overleaf)

Taken on the path from Inverkirkaig, this picture shows clearly the surprising length, and the sharp undulations, of Suilven's summit ridge.

The locked boat on Fionn Loch

The southern approach to Suilven involves a long drive round the coast from Lochinver, followed by a trudge round Fionn Loch. But time can be saved if the climber arranges to take this locked boat across to the base of the gully which gives access to the Bealach Mor – the dip in the ridge which is also reached from the north.

Canisp from a ridge lochan

Climbers making the traverse of Suilven for the
first time may well be surprised and enchanted
to discover this tiny lochan on such a narrow
ridge.

Meall Mheadhonach
from Caisteal Liath

hough this peak presents no problems to
perienced mountaineers, mountain walkers
ould not attempt the ascent of the great
nnacle shown here, since any slip would mean
fall of some 2,000 feet. But the middle section
the ridge, and even the ascent of Caisteal
ath (from which this picture was taken) are
latively easy, and the Castle offers a
apendous panorama that includes the sea and
astline – though, to my mind, this view is the
ost breathtaking.

Kylesku Ferry

This famous ferry plies the waters of three beautiful lochs – Loch Cairnbawn, Loch Glencoul and Loch Glendhui – that come together at Kylesku in some of the wildest country in Sutherland. In my early days no charge was made for the ferry, but the increase in tourist traffic put an end to that! A bridge is now under construction and approach roads on either side have already been completed.

Loch Glendhui from Kylesku

This large loch runs due east from the ferry,
and is famous for its brilliant reflection of the
sunrise. But its still waters also mirror the
silvery clouds, as seen here.

Quinag from Loch Cairnbawn

(overleaf)

The ferry runs from Kylesku to Kylestrome on Loch Cairnbawn, overlooked by the two northern spurs of Quinag. On the left is Sail Gharbh, and a clear morning's light reveals the famous Barrel Buttress between deep, nearly vertical gullies. The ascent of this buttress is one of the most difficult climbs in the region.

Scotch mist

This picture is included to convince correspondents that I do not always enjoy perfect weather for my work. Ben Stack was photographed from the road descending to Laxford Bridge in June 1982, when dense mist had hung over the landscape for days on end. During the month I spent in the Highlands on this trip, there were only two days when I could clearly see and photograph the hills.

A distant view of Foinaven

(overleaf)

This group of hills, straddling vast moorland solitudes in the north of Sutherland, is too remote to become popular with mountain walkers. During the drive from Scourie, Foinaven suddenly appears on the distant horizon (as seen here), but it can only be reached by crossing immense tracts of bog from a point some miles to the north of Rhiconich.

Ganu Mor from Foinaven ridge

(overleaf pp 148/149)

Foinaven consists entirely of quartzite, and the flat-topped peak seen in this picture is the highest of the five that deck the ridge.

A' Cheir Ghorm

This prominent spur extends northwards from
the main ridge of Foinaven, and is badly
eroded. To sit alone on its crest, as I have done,
and hear disintegrated blocks of quartzite
falling, is one of the most eerie experiences I
have had on the mountains of Britain.

Glen Affric

(overleaf)

The public road to this world-famous glen begins in Strath Glass and follows Chisholm's Pass above the Dog Falls to the eastern end of Loch Benevian, seen here. Glen Affric should be visited, if possible, in the autumn, when millions of gold-leaved birches make a glorious picture.

Two elegant birches

These isolated trees illustrate to perfection the
way the pure gold of autumn contrasts with the
waters of the loch and its background of dark
pines.

Loch Benevian

(overleaf)

The beauty of this glorious loch is owed in part to the absence of the lateral moraine that mars so many of Britain's lakes. This is because the waters of Loch Mullardoch in the adjoining Glen Cannich flow through a tunnel into Glen Affric and automatically 'top up' Loch Benevian – a clever idea developed by the Scottish Hydro-electric Board. Raising the level of the loch has meant abandoning the old road along its shore.

The cliffs of Cairn Lochan

The cliffs of this great corrie, part of the Cairn Gorm range, are perhaps the most magnificent in the region. (This long ridge and its corries can be seen in plates 156/7 in *Scotland*.) Mountain walkers can reach the cairn on Cairn Gorm by the chairlift in Coire Cas, and from there can enjoy a splendid walk along the crest of Stob Coire an t'Sneachda to the cairn on the very edge of Cairn Lochan, where precipitous cliffs enclose Coire an Lochain with two tiny lochans at their base. As the cliffs face northwest, the spectacular scene can only be satisfactorily photographed when they are lit by the declining sun.

Snow

(overleaf)

Immediately to the west of the summit of Cairn Lochan the snow accumulates throughout the winter. When the temperature rises, the lower section of snow breaks away and falls through the Vent, a narrow opening in the vertical cliffs below, then slides down across the immense face of the Great Sloping Slab to the two lochans below.

Invercauld Bridge

Though the River Dee, rising near the summit of Braeriach, at first threads its way through the wild and desolate Cairngorms, it later ripples through some of the most beautiful wooded stretches of Scotland. Invercauld Bridge, spanning the Dee between Braemar and Balmoral, has one of the loveliest settings of all, with the great mass of Lochnagar as a superb backdrop.

A stormy day on the Storr

(overleaf)

Clear weather in Skye reveals the Storr's
immense cliffs in detail, but this blustery June
morning provided a fast-moving, thunderous
cloud canopy instead.

The Old Man of Storr

This isolated 160-foot pinnacle of undercut trap rock defied rock-climbers for years. But in June 1955 it was climbed for the first time by D. Whillans, T. Barber and G. T. Sutton, who before abseiling down left a coin on the summit. As far as I know, it is still there.

A collection of strange pinnacles

Weird pinnacles and fantastic buttresses are an
unusual feature of the Storr, and climbers
should walk into the Sanctuary to see them.
Such a visit always induces in me a creepy
feeling of being watched by invisible, long-dead
occupants.

The Storr Needle

This slim, leaning pinnacle rises just behind the
Old Man, and at the time of writing it has yet
to be climbed.

The Quiraing Needle

(overleaf)

From afar this bizarre collection of rocks looks like a long, uninteresting rock wall frowning down on the lochan-strewn moorland near Staffin Bay. But on closer viewing it is found to be the most extraordinary collection of grotesque pinnacles and buttresses in Britain. The 100-foot Needle shown here was not climbed until August 1977, when a $16\frac{1}{2}$-year-old youth called Kevin R. Bridges finally reached the top.

Looking down on the Needle

A sketchy track climbs the wide gully behind
the Needle, from which it can be seen to
advantage, together with the Prison below it.
On the distant skyline rise the peaks of the
long, undulating, Trotternish ridge.

The Table

This surprising feature of Quiraing is hidden away on high, surrounded by rock columns, pinnacles, and the perpendicular wall of Meall nan Suireamach. Oval in shape, covered in sheep-cropped grass of vivid hue, and utterly deserted, it might make a gigantic putting green in one of the most spectacular amphitheatres in the country.

Snow on the Blaven ridges

(overleaf)

Motorists on Skye will enjoy the drive to Elgol because it opens up some of the most magnificent scenery on the island. Blaven, seen here across Loch Slapin, its ridges dappled with spring snow, is one of the finest views. The summit ridge, together with Clach Glas on the right, offer the rock-climber a traverse of great interest.

The southern Coolins and Camasunary

(overleaf pp 180/181)

A grand walk can be taken over the hills from the Elgol road near Kirkibost to Camasunary, the deserted shooting-lodge seen in the distant valley. This picture was taken from the highest point of the walk and shows the southern peaks of the Coolins, with Gars-bheinn prominent on the left, and Loch Scavaig below. Camasunary featured in Mary Stewart's novel, *Wildfire at Midnight*.

The northern Coolins

(overleaf pp 182/183)

This picture was taken from the same viewpoint as the previous plate, and reveals a distant view of Sgurr nan Gillean on the extreme right of the ridge.

The Cioch

Sron na Ciche is the most important climbing-
ground in the Coolins, and is easily reached
from Glen Brittle. The Cioch, seen here, is a
favourite climb: it is a large boss of rock
projecting from the main, vertical line of cliffs
which enclose Coire Lagan. When my
companions reached the summit, I lay down on
the narrow escarpment in the foreground to
photograph them. I had to change a lens, but
the rucksack on my back was jammed in a
groove – very careful wriggles were necessary if
I was to reach it without falling 1,000 feet
down the cliffs to my right. I managed it safely,
and this is the result.

Glen Brittle youth hostel

Having crossed the lofty Skye moorland from
Sligachan, the road runs along the valley bottom
to its terminus at the campsite. The youth
hostel is one of the most popular on the island,
and to illustrate better its lonely situation in this
remote glen, I scrambled up the lower slopes of
the Coolins.

Sgurr nan Gobhar

(overleaf)

This little peak terminates the lofty spur that falls downward from Sgurr na Banachdich, and since it is opposite the youth hostel climbers use it as a safe and easy ascent to the main ridge. It is an attractive route, looking down on Coire Ghreadaidh on the left and Coire na Banachdich on the right.

A region of waterfalls

(overleaf p 189)

As the path climbs for some distance alongside a turbulent burn, it passes several attractive waterfalls. The one seen here is the third.

Coire na Banachdich

This shot, taken from Glen Brittle, is included to show the position of Sgurr nan Gobhar, a spur which rises on the left and encloses the corrie.

Sgurr nan Gobhar from the campsite

(overleaf)

The campsite in Glen Brittle has a splendid view of the undulating ridge of this peak. Its traverse presents no difficulties, and is reminiscent of Striding Edge on Helvellyn.

The campsite from Loch Brittle

Coire Lagan and its enclosing peaks dominate the peaceful picture (which was taken with a telephoto lens) of this popular campsite by the shores of the loch.

Snow on the northern Coolins

(overleaf)

This scene, familiar to climbers who love Skye, was taken from the small lochan on the left of the Carbost road just above Sligachan: it shows Sgurr nan Gillean prominent on the left, with the peaks on its right huddled together as far as Bruach na Frithe.

Gillean from the south-east ridge

(overleaf pp 198/199)

Climbers making for the summit by the tourist route will see it rearing up like a cathedral tower when they reach the south-east ridge. The safe route keeps to the left, with slopes plummeting down to Lota Corrie; and the climber must use his hands for the final ascent to the cairn. On a clear day, the panorama from the summit is one of the finest in Skye, with the sea visible in every direction. In this picture, the Pinnacle Ridge can be seen on the right, and the ridge twisting away to the left eventually reaches Alasdair, the highest peak in the Coolins.

The western ridge of Gillean

The descent of this ridge is more difficult than
the ascent, described in the previous caption,
because it includes the passing of the Policeman,
a vertical obelisk of rock seemingly poised in
space. In this picture, the highest peak in the
background is Bruach na Frithe.

Gillean seen through clouds

This is an unusual portrait of Gillean and its satellites, for in years of visits to Skye I have only seen such a wreath of clouds on one occasion.

A Skye sunset

(overleaf)

This sunset developed as I was changing for dinner in my room at the Sligachan Hotel. I put on my dressing-gown and sallied forth to make sure of the shot!